Women Marrying Younger Men: A Biblical Perspective

. . . With breakthrough counsels that will save you from making the wrong decision.

Ebenezer Afolabi

DEDICATION

I want to dedicate this book to my Lord and Saviour, Jesus Christ. He is the solid rock upon which I stand and my ever-present help in times of trouble. To Him be glory forevermore. Also to every true lovers who are considering entering such a unique relationship where the *woman is older than the man.*

To my wife, my friend and confidant, Kikelomo. Thanks for all your support, love and prayers.

I am very grateful to you.

Table of Contents

Preface

Preface

All my efforts to get Christian materials which address the subject women marrying younger men proved abortive. I tried hard to see if any scholar or writer had made any contribution to the subject, but all I found were advices – good advices though – but no one seems to address the subject from the biblical perspective. Although, what actually motivated me to embark on this somewhat challenging task was the question a young lady flung online, seeking at least single reference in the Bible where a woman married a younger man.

She was in love with a younger man and she didn't want to lose the young man at all, but the parents of the young man demanded that she provides a place in the Bible where such a marriage can be supported; otherwise they will not give their consents. Her attempts to find a place in the Bible to support her "unique" love affair was abortive and she threw the question open to everyone online. To my amazement, no one was able to provide at least a passage from the scripture to support the subject. I felt there should be answer somewhere and I started searching my Bible to see the possibility of such or at least something close to that.

Interestingly after a long search into the scriptures, I was able to come up with an answer—not from a single passage, but passages that might take us closer to what we are looking for. I took the pains to do this because I am sure she is not the only one having the same challenge. Trust me; I am not trying to develop the doctrine of women marrying younger men from the passages I have discovered. I am not giving the Church a new marital doctrine; I am only trying to help young folks who are into such union and who may be asking the same question this lady asked.

My focus is to actually create a balance here and to help those who are in such relationships to get things right. Therefore, this book is not meant for those women who are just hanging around younger men just for the fun of it or merely to use the younger men as 'sex machines'. This is not a book for toy boys or trophy wives. I am addressing those who are hoping to go into a lifelong marital relationship and who are sincerely seeking advice before they go deeper into the relationship.

However, this book intends to answer three pivotal questions. The questions are briefly highlighted below:

1. What is actually wrong with such a union?

2. Is there any guarantee for success in such a union or everyone should expect problems in the long-run?

3. What does the Bible have to say about this kind of marriage?

However, for the sake of convenience, "Women Marrying Younger Men" shall subsequently be expressed with this abbreviation: W.M.Y.M. Thereafter, the author shall express his reservations and offer some advice that will help couples or the intending couples not to regret their decisions. Come with me as I make my opinion known through this book. Make sure you pay rapt attention as you read through the pages of this book. Thank you.

Ebenezer Afolabi

CHAPTER 1

Does Age Really Matter?

The idea of women marrying younger men is becoming popular in our days, but its social and cultural acceptability has been strongly challenged. It is not really a big deal in some parts of the world, but it is a big deal in some places in Africa. We see several cases of WMYM among movie stars, musicians, athletes and celebrities. It is a strange and unacceptable idea in Africa and everyone seem to envisage nothing but problems in such union. In Africa, this kind of relationship faces rejections, oppositions and mockery because people feel such relationship is against norm and it should not be accepted at all. Some people even choose to call it a *taboo*.

However, things are changing, paradigms are challenged and values have been distorted in the name of freedom. Relativism has taken the place of the absolute, and the doctrine of "autonomous self" is gaining dominance in the world we live in today. People clamour for freedom but the question is: is freedom the permission to do what we *want* to do or it is the liberty to do what we *ought* to do? In my opinion, I think the latter is correct. Freedom is the liberty to do what ought to be done.

In regard to age differences between couples in marriage, what is the ideal? Is there any standard to follow in regard to age differences among couples? Does age really change anything or affect anything?

Put succinctly, it is a generally accepted norm in almost every human society that men (husbands) should be older than their wives. Men generally want to marry younger women and women would generally prefer to marry older men too. This is not because God gave any specific instruction regarding this, but it has been an acceptable practice among men throughout history.

According to 2012 Census Bureau data, 85.9 per cent of husbands are older than or about the same age as their wives. That leaves 14.2 per cent of all husbands who are at least two years younger than their wives. 2013 US Population Survey provides an explicit survey (see table in the next page):

Age difference in heterosexual married couples, 2013 US Population Survey.[1]

Statistics

Age difference	Percentage of All Married Couples
Husband 20+ years older than wife	1.0
Husband 15–19 years older than wife	1.6
Husband 10–14 years older than wife	4.8
Husband 6–9 years older than wife	11.6
Husband 4–5 years older than wife	13.3
Husband 2–3 years older than wife	20.4
Husband and wife within 1 year	33.2

Wife 2–3 years older than husband	6.5
Wife 4–5 years older than husband	3.3
Wife 6–9 years older than husband	2.7
Wife 10–14 years older than husband	1.0
Wife 15–19 years older than husband	0.3
Wife 20+ years older than husband	0.3

Many have argued that in an ideal situation, husbands should be older than their wives because God created the man first and that should be the standard we all must follow in marriage. Yes, they are right by saying God created the man first and He made him the head of the family. But may I ask you to tell me the age difference between

Adam and Eve. I guess you cannot be so sure and I believe God did not create any other thing after the sixth day. Therefore, Adam and Eve could have been created the same day—although one might still be older than the other since they were not created the same minute. So Adam could have been some hours older than Eve. That is by the way.

Like I said earlier, it is a generally accepted norm that men should be older than their wives. But what should be the age difference between them? No specific age difference is given in the Bible. I am not referring to the age a man or woman should marry now, but what should be the age gap between two eligible individuals who plans to get married to each other?

New research shows that, at least for the Sami people of preindustrial Finland, men should marry a woman almost 15 years their junior to maximize their chances of having the most offspring that survive.[2] Most men marry women younger than they are; with the difference being between two and three years in Spain, the UK reporting the difference to be on average about three years, and the US, two and a half.[3] From the report above, it is certain that there is no uniform view as to what should be the age difference between couples, but the general norm remains that the male partner is expected to be older than the female.

In *The Autobiography of Malcolm X* published in the 1950s, Nation of Islam leader Elijah Muhammad taught that a wife's ideal age was half the man's age plus seven; this age gap should make up for women's maturing more quickly than men, as well as ensure that the husband was sufficiently authoritative over his wife.[4] Although Elijah Muhammad's view seems superficial, but it shows the general perspective of the people within his religious tradition.

A similar view is also held by Africans—the view that men should be significantly older than their wives to ensure that the husband is sufficiently authoritative over his wife. Surprisingly, the half-your-age plus seven rule has found its way into our cultural lexicon. It has been popularized and it is *almost* becoming the standard rule for age disparity among couples.

The reason for supporting the idea that a man should marry a woman younger than him has been a subject of significant discussion among behavioural Psychologists and experts in the field of Sociology. Ecologist Samuli Helle of the University of Turku in Finland maintains: "We found that marrying women 14.6 years younger maximized men's lifetime reproductive success—in other words, the number of offspring surviving to age 18."[5]

Like I said earlier, WMYM may not really be a serious issue in the western society because of the "anything goes" kind of life that has been embraced in the western culture and the freedom of choice the constitution had given everyone. But even if it is a serious issue, what role is age playing in marriage?

Age in my opinion is not one of the major factors that determine whether a marriage will be successful or not. It does play a significant role, no doubt, but in true friendship, age does not really count. No one lays strong emphasis on who is older in true friendship. Rather, the individuals involved in the friendship relates freely, not emphasizing seniority or superiority. This should be the same in the marriage where love reigns.

Age does not *always* determine headship in every human society. It is the role the individual *recognized* as the head plays at the given time that makes him or her leader. For instance, I am a Pastor; a young pastor, and at least 60 per cent of my congregation are far older than me, yet I am the head. I am the head (the leader) simply because of the role I play in the church, not because I am older than them all. The same goes to the marriage where the wife is older than her husband.

In this kind of marriage, the man still plays the role of a husband while the woman plays the role of a wife. No one can reverse the order. No matter the age difference, no culture, tradition or people will ever give the role of a husband to the woman because she is older.

The man does not become the husband because he is older; although can give him some measures of authority in the home, but age does not confer headship on him. He is the husband because he is the man of the house and that automatically makes him the head.

In this kind of situation, the duo comes into the marital relationship, not with the intention of reversing the marital order by giving the headship of the family to the woman because she is older, but both comes into the relationship with the knowledge that the man maintains his headship no matter the age disparity. In fact, the duo must first come to an agreement with each other before entering the relationship that the "age clause" that exists between them *will never* tamper with whom should be the head of the family, neither will it become a matter of discussion whenever conflict arises in the family. When all of the above is taken into consideration, success is guaranteed.

Therefore, age does not determine the success of any marriage; it is maturity, love, trust, respect, patience and understanding that determine the success of any marriage. Age is just the chronological gap between the two people.

Have you counted the Cost?

Can you just wait a moment to count the cost of venturing into this "unique" relationship before you finalize your decision? Even if you think you feel good with such relationship, isn't it good to wait a minute to count the cost? Please don't get me wrong; I do not say it is morally wrong for a woman to marry a younger man, but I think it is advisable for both parties to critically count the cost first. I understand that love transcends all the mockeries, rejections and any ugly thing you might face; yet there is need for critical consideration.

The two important questions you must ask yourself are: can I stand some of the inevitable challenges that come with my decision to marry a younger man or an older lady? Am I willing to keep my commitment to this marriage intact even when the inevitable challenges arise? These two questions are crucial and fundamental to the decision you are about to make.

CHAPTER 2

Excuses for Rejecting WMYM

The excuses people give for rejecting the idea of women marrying younger men (cougar marriage as some would call it) are enormous but few shall be discussed below.

1. Cultural Excuses: "It is against our culture and tradition", they often say. People tend to disagree with such union when it is not an acceptable practice within their cultures. To make things worse for the lovers, the people would announce a terrible tragedy that might befall anyone who acts contrary to the acceptable norms within that culture.

Cultural beliefs may be a major barrier to such a unique relationship as this. However, some cultures are more flexible than the others. But in some cases, cultural beliefs might be one of the strongest barriers against WMYM. Along with the cultural beliefs of the people involved in this union is the *Consensus Gentium* of the people within the culture where the relationship is taking place. *Consensus Gentium* is from the Latin word meaning 'the agreement of the people'. It is an ancient criterion for decision making among a group of people who practices the same culture. *Consensus Gentium* is also referred to as the climate of opinion, community sentiment, general belief, conventional wisdom, prevailing sentiment, etc. *Consensus Gentium* therefore carries a weight of authority in decision making, especially among those who have cultural affiliations. Consequently, if the union is against the community sentiment or the general belief of the people where the union is taking place, they may likely raise their eyebrows against the union.

2. Religious Excuse: Like I said in the preface of the young lady who was deeply in love with a younger man, the mother of the young man insisted that they would never marry each other because she can't find a place in the Bible to support such a union. The lady voiced out to the world to see if anyone could actually help her find a place in the Bible to support her relationship with her lover and to convince her mother-in-law. This was a serious challenge for her. This experience is not peculiar to her alone. There are several others having similar challenges simply because it is against their religious beliefs.

Religion is indeed a strong factor in this kind of union. Therefore, if such a union is against the ethos of their religious faith, it might be challenged, discouraged and ultimately disallowed.

3. Physiological Excuse: If you are a woman and you marry a younger man, you will soon look older than him, and he may not be attracted to you again. That's the assumption of many people. For the woman, she may have to put in more efforts to be able to meet the sexual need of her husband. She returns home very tired after a very hectic day, she gets into the kitchen to prepare dinner for her family, and her husband also needs her in bed. You can imagine how tired she would be after a very hectic day and also attending to domestic works, and yet, her husband needs her in bed.

Research has shown that men want sex three times more than women. He wants it almost every other day, but she is too tired and her husband is demanding for it. As her age increases, her strength begins to decline. In some cases, sexual intercourse can even become painful for older women, and stress may lead to frigidity. Stress makes sex life suffer; it can lower your sex drive. However, medical scientists are doing great jobs in helping older people to continue to experience an active sex life.

Nevertheless, the assumption of some people is that, if for any reason she could not meet her husband's sexual need, she may have to share her husband with a younger lady somewhere. Aside that, some people feel older women may not be as romantic and sexy as young ladies would. These assumptions had greatly been contested by medical experts, but when we look at the matter holistically, the two parties (those who believe older women are not romantic and those who say they are sexually active even at old ages) are making sensible points—it's just a matter of perspectives. As she gets older you begin to notice wrinkles on her face, her breasts becoming saggy, and other physiological changes that may vastly make younger men to prefer younger ladies to older ones begin to occur in her.

These are some of the physiological excuses people give for discouraging such a peculiar union. These excuses may look flimsy to some people but I feel there is still need for a critical consideration of the whole matter.

4. **Attitudinal Excuse:** This is an excuse that she may not be submissive to her younger husband. I personally believe that submission and respect are not the functions of age; they are issues which bother on individual's

personalities. Although the consciousness of the age difference that exists among the two lovers may sometimes affect their attitudes toward each other, but I counsel that the older woman should be ready to give up her age, so to speak, and willingly accept the headship of her younger man and the man must not be threatened by the age of his wife. Both of them must exhibit mutual respect for each other in the relationship.

Nevertheless, she must always remember that she is not his *mother* or big sister, but his wife. If she had agreed to be the wife of the younger man, then she must put on the attitude of submission, humility and respect for her younger man.

5. Sociological Excuse: This is an excuse that she may not really be as social as younger ladies would. They will definitely have different social preferences, no doubt about that. Apart from that, will the young man really be comfortable with the friends of his older wife who are of the same age group with her? What about the lady; will she be comfortable staying around the friends of his younger man? These are some of the excuses people often give for rejecting such a unique union—I call it a "unique union".

A young man once wrote to me to seek my counsel concerning his desire to marry an older lady. They obviously love each other but the young man doesn't have enough courage to continue the relationship because of people's opinions about the relationship. He belongs to a culture where a woman marrying younger men is seldom embraced. For this reason, he decided to end the relationship.

I tried to make him understand that he is not going to marry for the people and people's opinions about the marriage doesn't really count, but he lacked the courage to continue. Perhaps you are reading this book and that's exactly how you feel about your relationship with your older lady. If you are truly in love with her and you are truly convinced you are meant for each other, people's opinions should never make you feel uncomfortable or want to opt out of the relationship. If you end the relationship only because of what friends think of the relationship, you have only demonstrated weakness and insincerity (your love isn't genuine in the first place.

Your ability to stay in the relationship in spite of what anybody feels about you and the relationship shows strong-will, sincerity, and courage. Do you really love the guy? Stay with him. Are you truly in love with the lady? Don't call it a quit. Except there are other factors that you both are sure will never make the relationship work, do not call it a quit because of the biases and sentiments of friends.

CHAPTER 3

Is the Bible in Support of WMYM?

Can we find any passage to support WMYM in the Bible? This is the second question this book shall attempt to answer. This is my motivation for writing this book. Many have asked and are still asking this same question and I am willing to make my opinion known to you in this chapter.

Is there any possibility for WMYM in the Bible? Put succinctly, YES! I guess that is strange to you. "But I can't find anything like that in the Bible", you say. Surprisingly, I have found some. I will show you in a moment. Just go along with me.

The Bible is neither against WMYM nor in support of it. However, we have the possibility of WMYM in the Bible, but this is only possible within the context of "levirate marriage" or what is called *yibbum* in Judaism.

Understanding Levirate Marriage

Levirate marriage is a primitive practice among the Jews, some African tribes and in some oriental cultures. In Biblical law, a matrimonial relationship is established between a widow whose husband died without having had children and the brother of the deceased who is obligated to marry her. This is the levirate act.[1] Ordinarily speaking, it is unacceptable and immoral for a man to have any sexual relationship with his brother's wife according to the Law of Moses, but it is required in levirate marriage for the sake of raising progeny for the deceased brother.

The levirate custom makes provision for a man who died without male descendants to carry on his name. The custom requires his surviving brother or a close relative to marry the widow of his deceased brother for the purpose of raising an offspring for him and *the first son* would then be attributed to the brother who had died. In some cases, this child is named after the deceased brother. The brother who marries the widow of his dead brother is called *levir* in Latin, which means "brother-in-law."

In Deuteronomy 25:5, Moses said, "If brothers are living together and one of them dies without a son, his widow must not marry outside the family. Her husband's brother shall take her and marry her and fulfil the duty of a brother-in-law to her" (NIV). This is the levirate law provided by Moses.

Although the Torah provides no clear reason for levirate marriage, but the purpose was clearly defined among the ancient Jews. The Torah simply states that the levirate marriage ensures that the name of the deceased is not totally blotted out in Israel. According to Blaine Robison, "The primary purpose of the *yibbum* law was to preserve the dead man's name in Israel and insure that assets belonging to him and the widow remained in the family to be passed on to the son."[2]

The levirate tradition predated the Law of Moses. We have the first instance recorded in Genesis 38. Genesis 38:6-8 records:

> Judah got a wife for Er, his firstborn, and her name was Tamar. But Er, Judah's firstborn, was wicked in the LORD's sight; so the LORD put him to death. Then

Judah said to Onan, "Lie with your brother's wife and fulfil your duty to her as a brother-in-law to produce offspring for your brother." But Onan knew that the offspring would not be his; so whenever he lay with the brother's wife, he spilled his semen on the ground to keep from producing offspring for his brother. What he did was wicked in the LORD's sight; so he put him to death also . . . .

From the passage above we could see that the custom of levirate marriage has been in practice even before Moses made it a Law in Deuteronomy 25.

So what does WMYM have to do with Levirate Marriage?

I guess you are wondering if the story of Judah and his three sons have anything to do with WMYM. It is true that the passage does not hold any teaching on the subject; neither was it taught by Moses the lawgiver.

Like I said earlier, although there is no single passage in the entire Bible which addresses the subject or make any allusion to it, but there is the possibility of such within the context of levirate marriage. Let's take a critical look at Genesis 38 again, reading from the sixth verse.

Judah had three sons: Er, Onan, and Shelah. Er married Tamar, but Er was wicked in the LORD's sight, so the LORD put him to death. Therefore by custom, Onan should marry Tamar, the widow of his deceased brother, in order to fulfil his duty to her as a brother-in-law to produce offspring for his brother Er. Onan also did what was wicked before the LORD, so the LORD put him to death too. Since Onan could not produce an offspring for his late brother, then Tamar should be given to Shelah to marry.

Now carefully look at what Judah said in verse 11: "Judah then said to his daughter-in-law Tamar, "Live as a widow in your father's house *until* my son *Shelah grows up.*"

(emphasis mine). This text suggests to us that Shelah would have been younger than Tamar, but custom makes it mandatory for Shelah to marry Tamar. My paraphrase: Judah said to Tamar, relax! The young man will perform the duty of a brother-in-law to you, but he is still very young for that now. Live in your father's house *until my son Shelah grows up*. The Living Bible puts it this way: "Then Judah told Tamar, his daughter-in-law, not to marry again at the time, but to return to her childhood home and to her parents, and to remain a widow there until his youngest son, Shelah, was old enough to marry her. . . ." Take a critical look at the text again. It is crystal clear that Tamar would have been older than Shelah if they eventually got married.

Our second example is found in the gospel of Luke. Luke 20:27-36 records a fantastic discussion between the Sadducees and Jesus.

It is also about the levirate marriage. The Sadducees quoted Deuteronomy 25:5, and sought Jesus' opinion on the text. Let's go through the discussion carefully. Verses 29 to 31 reads: "Now there were seven brothers. The first one married a woman and died childless. The second and then the third married her, and in the same way the seven died, leaving no children."

You will notice from the story that Jesus never told the Sadducees that such marriage is wrong—I mean levirate marriage. Jesus accepted the Jewish custom of levirate marriage. Here is the point: We do not have a command in the Bible regarding the age gap that should be between husbands and wives. However, for the sake of this discussion, let's make Abraham and Sarah our case study.

Abraham was ten years older than Sarah. Genesis 17:17 reads: "Abraham fell facedown; he laughed and said to himself, "Will a son be born to a man a hundred years old? Will Sarah bear a child at the age of ninety?" So let's take the age difference between Abraham and Sarah as the standard couples followed in the Bible days. In other words, we want to assume that in their days, a man must or should be at least ten years older than his wife. What about the age gaps between siblings? Now let's consider the age gaps that might be between children in Bible days.

We cannot be too sure of the age gaps between children in the Bible days, but let's take Moses and Aaron as the standard. Exodus 7:7 records that Aaron was three years older than Moses. So, for the sake of this discussion, let's assume that there were always three years intervals between siblings in the Bible days. Let's go back to Jesus' discussion with the Sadducees.

Let's assume that the first husband was ten years older than his wife. He had six younger brothers. He died childless and tradition requires that the immediate younger brother should marry the widow. By the assumption above, the immediate younger brother would be at least three years younger than his late brother, and the same goes on and on like that. If the woman could not have a child through the first of the six surviving brothers and he died also, she goes to the next until she has a child through any of the six brothers.

Let's assume that she bore no child for the first three out of the six brothers, and there were three years interval each between the brothers, then she would marry the fourth brother and the list could go on and on like that. Now imagine what would be the age difference between the woman and the fourth, fifth and the sixth brother. That means the woman would be eight years older than the sixth brother. Do you understand? Let me take you through the story again.

Her first husband was ten years older than her and he had six younger brothers. By our assumption, there were three years interval between each of them just like the case of Moses and Aaron in Exodus 7:7. If the first husband was ten years older than the wife, it follows that the first levir would be seven years older than the woman. The second levir would be four years older than her and the third levir would be a year older than her. By the time she gets to the fourth levir, the order would change and she will be two years older than him, five years older than the fifth levir, and eight years older than the sixth levir. Simply subtract three from ten in six places; the answer you get is minus eight. It is clear from the above that the woman would be eight years older than the sixth brother.

Therefore, to succinctly answer the question of the young lady, WMYM is only possible within the context of levirate marriage. However, like I said earlier, the Bible is neither in support nor against WMYM. The Bible is silent about the matter, but it is important that the two individuals planning to enter into such marital relationship should critically consider their choices and allow God to lead them.

CHAPTER 4

Is there any Guarantee for Success in the Marriage?

The success of any and every marriage depends on what the couple puts into it and allows in it. The duo must first make up their minds that the marriage must succeed irrespective of the age clause and must also endeavour to create the atmosphere that will ensure the success of the marriage—the atmosphere where love, empathy, trust, altruism, respect, honesty and humility thrives. The marriage *cannot* succeed if the atmosphere described above is not present in the family—even if there is no age clause between the couple.

I have seen some Christian couples who are doing just fine in their marriages in spite of the age clauses. They simply decided not to allow the age thing to be a problem to them. They kept strictly to the principles of success in marriage as taught in the Bible.

However, it is important for me to say this to the ladies and gentlemen who want to consider this kind of marriage that, the moment you feel you are not going to be comfortable and bold enough to introduce your partner to your friends (I do not mean telling everyone about the age clause), then it is better to take a pause and reconsider the choice you want to make. Furthermore, the moment any of you is no longer feeling comfortable and enthusiastic about the two of you coming together as marriage partners, it is better to reconsider your choices. First, carefully find out the reason for why he or she is not comfortable and the reason for lack of enthusiasm. Make sure you are sincere with each other and be sure your reason for considering marrying each other is nothing but love and the knowledge of God's will for your lives.

WMYM is just like any other marriage and it can be successful just like any other marriage, provided the foundation is not faulty. It also has its own challenges like every other marriage, and the couples in it can also have a heaven on earth experience, regardless of the age clause. Nevertheless, when the foundation is not built upon integrity and genuine love, it will inevitably fall.

When the foundation is built upon deception, self-centeredness, grubbiness, ego, illicit passion, lust and infatuation, it is just a matter of time; the marriage will soon fall and be ruined beyond repair.

Therefore, the success of the marriage depends to a large extent on what you and your partner puts into it and allows in it. The age clause in the marriage is never a barrier to the success of the marriage.

What do you expect?

What do you really expect from the relationship? Better put this way: what is the vision you have for your marriage regardless of the age clause? Is it to change your maiden name and raise kids, or to have a partner who is always there to meet your emotional and sexual needs? What do you want your marriage to look like? As a man, is your vision simply to have someone who could help you for laundry, do house chores, raise kids for you, and satisfy your sexual desires? What is actually the vision you have for your marriage? Why do you really need to get married? The success of your marriage could only be defined by what your vision is.

Several years ago when I was courting my wife, the Lord asked me to write down how I want my marriage to look like. I wrote it and presented it to God in prayer for Him to help me accomplish what I wrote. I can tell you that it is working for me today as envisioned.

The same question I am asking you now is the same question I ask any young person that comes to me to seek counsel in marriage. I always asked them what vision they have for their lives and the kind of home they want to have. This will guide and help them to make the right choice of marriage. If the man or the lady you want to marry does not fit into the vision God has given you for life and marriage, it is better you reconsider your choice.

Write down your vision and share them with your partner. Be sensitive to his or her reactions, ask questions, find out what he or she feels about the visions you both have, ask if both of you are willing and ready to work together for the fulfilment of those visions, and finally commit them to God in prayer.

However, don't just marry a husband or a wife; marry a dream partner. *Marry someone whose dreams and visions are compatible with yours.* And you must understand that marital compatibility doesn't always mean resemblance. Your personalities may not have any resemblance. Your tastes may not be the same, your emotional make-up may not be the same, your worldview may differ — that is, you may not always reason alike. All of that does not mean you are not compatible. Compatibility speaks more of complementing each other than seeking resemblance in each other.

CHAPTER 5

My Reservations

I really want to express my reservations for this kind of marriage. I have read several blog posts on the subject of WMYM; they all claimed to be deeply in love with one another, but I think there is still need for thoughtful considerations in this matter.

In some of the posts I read earlier, and from some of my personal interactions with some men and ladies, some women are married to men who are 15 years, 17 years, 20 years, and even 24 years younger than them. I think such age gaps are outrageous, crazy, ridiculous and weird. I perceive that in most cases, what could lead to such outrageous age clause includes lust, infatuation, frustration, wrong self-judgment, selfishness and greed. These wide age gaps raise a lot of questions in my mind.

From my observations, I deduce that *most* (not all) of the men who agreed to go into this kind of marriage are up to something. Perhaps the women have what they are desperately in need of, so they agreed to marry the older women. In most cases, it is the older woman that carries the greatest burden and pays the highest price to ensure the marriage works. Because of the fear of losing her younger husband to younger ladies on the street, she is willing to give the marriage all that it takes, even to the point of going out of her way to make sure the marriage works.

The early days of the marriage may look rosy and fantastic, but as years pass by, the young man's eyes are suddenly opened to the ageing physique of his older wife and as a result, the older spouse may no longer look appealing to him after noticing those apparent changes.

As she's growing older, her face begins to get wrinkled, her breasts start to droop, she begins to experience mood swings, and a lot of physiological changes will begin to take place in her body. Can you imagine how a woman who is 15 years older than her husband will be when these changes become obvious? A study had shown that women who are seven to nine years older than their husbands have a 20 per cent higher mortality rate than if they were the same age.

Come on! Let's be realistic; such age gaps (10, 15, 20 age disparities) are crazy and ridiculous. They may both enjoy the euphoria of love in the early days of their marriage, but as years passes by, these realities will be done on both of them. Remember the old saying: "If love is a dream, marriage is the alarm clock."

However, I understand that love transcends all these inadequacies, but we must never deny the reality of these changes. Nevertheless, the marriage can still work in spite of the vast age differences, but more effort is required.

It is seriously important that the duo should carefully count the cost of venturing into this relationship, and not be carried away by the fantastic illusions which surround love.

I am not trying to dethrone love. Love is a key and indispensable factor which determines the success of any marriage. However, there is need for the intending couple to *consider* their choices carefully.

Therefore this is my submission: there is nothing morally wrong with women marrying younger men, if they both feel good about it. What matters is love and understanding. If you are in it already and you feel okay with it, go ahead and enjoy the cruise. If you are just coming into it, consider your choice critically and allow God to guide you. If you are deeply and sincerely in love with each other, but the female counterpart is older and you are confused if the Bible supports such a practice, I think I have been able to help you answer your question. The Bible does not give us any instruction regarding WMYM and I do not think the scriptures frowns at it. It is all your choice, but your choice needs to be given a critical consideration.

As a believer, you must allow God to lead you in every decision you want to make and you must always seek His will for your life— these include marriage, career, ministry, etc.

According to Romans 12:2, God's will is God, acceptable and perfect. He is willing to lead and guide you. He doesn't want you to make wrong choice of marriage. Seek His will and you will be happy for it.

CHAPTER 6

My Advice to Older Ladies

I think it is needful for me to sound this warning to intending couples before they dabble into the marriage. This is not to scare you at all; trust me. I am doing this because many people go into such marriage blindly and for many reasons without necessarily finding out what is required for the success of the marriage. Below are some of the advices I have to offer older ladies who are considering marrying younger men:

1. Do not go into the relationship out of frustration or desperation. Many of the ladies who go into this kind of relationship do so simply because of frustration and desperation. Perhaps they think they are growing older and no man is proposing to marry them. They felt they may remain unmarried if they refuse any man who proposes to marry them. As a result, they accept to marry any man who comes their ways and who seems to be meeting their emotional needs.

Another reason why older ladies sometimes agree to marry younger men can be due to their past ugly experiences. Perhaps they've once loved and trusted some guys who jilted them. This can make them consent to marry younger men whom they felt are responsible and can possibly fill the vacuum their 'exes' left in their lives. Sometimes these younger men are given the chance to come into their lives to merely play a substitutionary role. Ladies, please do not marry out of frustration or desperation. If you agree to marry a guy because of frustration, you may end up marrying a mere 'service provider' and not a loving husband.

A service provider is only there to meet your emotional and sexual needs. Having rendered the service for which you allowed him into your life, what happens next? Think about that. Marrying out of frustration or desperation is unhealthy and can be hazardous.

2. **Do not go into the relationship for sexual or emotional satisfactions only**. Some ladies are of the opinion that younger men are more sexually active and romantic than older men. This may not be true in all cases. Having sexual satisfaction has more to do with

enlightenment and experience. It is possible for a younger man to have more strength and energy that the older ones, but if he lacks the skills involved in giving sexual satisfaction, he may just expend his energy and still not satisfy his woman. That is by the way. There are more to love and marriage than sex.

Sex will not and cannot give you all the satisfactions you will ever need in a relationship. There are several ups and downs in marriage and many unforeseen problems that might come to test your love and commitment to each other. If all that brought you into the relationship is simply to satisfy your sexual fantasies, you may regret ever making the choice to be married in the first place. Marriage is interesting. You can have heaven-on-earth experience in your marriage if it is built on a solid foundation and it can be hellish if the foundation is faulty. On what foundation are you building your marriage? Are you building on the foundation of Christ and His word or on lust, lies, dishonesty and greed?

3. **Carefully weigh the pros and the cons before you say "I do".** This calls for honesty to oneself. Every relationship has its own challenges and monsters to conquer. Therefore, before you go too far, before he takes you to the altar, before you say "I do", it is important for you to critically and honestly consider the pros and the cons of your decision before going into the union. Do not think it will be rosy all through the way. Every marriage has its roses and thorns—especially the kind of marriage we are talking about—it has its own share of problems and its peculiarity will inevitably open it up to several challenges.

For instance, a research postulates that women who marry men seven to nine years their juniors have a 20 per cent higher mortality risk than women who marry their own age. Marrying a younger man may keep your feeling young, but he might be difficult to relate with on the other hand—especially when the gap is a vast one. Because of the age disparity, both of you may not share many common life experiences and it may be difficult to find common ground to stand on sometimes.

I am of the opinion that there are certain things books will *never* teach you; it takes age and experience to know them. Therefore, older ladies or women may have some difficulties in relating with their younger men at some points in life. My candid advice to those involved in this kind of relationship is to weigh the beautiful and the ugly sides of the union carefully before diving into it.

4. Never compare him with your ex. considering your age, it is possible that you may have been into some relationships in the past, and with each of this past relationships comes different emotional, social or sexual experiences. Perhaps the younger man seems not to measure up to the standard of your ex or exes in some areas; it is unhealthy to compare him with them. You must be willing to accept him as he is and patiently work *with* him until he could meet *some* of your expectations—do not expect him to meet all your expectations. Expecting him to meet all your expectations may not be realistic. You must never try to manipulate him to becoming who he is not.

5. Do not treat him like your younger brother; treat him as your husband. You must avoid the temptation of treating him like your younger brother. He is not your younger brother as far as marriage is concern. Although the age gap may be vast, but when it comes to marriage, the man assumes the responsibility of the head.

Regardless of the age difference between both of you, he deserves your respect and adoration. You must be submissive to him as a matter of necessity, so that both of you can have a joyous and enduring marital experiences.

I know the subject of submission in marriage has generated several arguments in many circles, but we must go by what the scripture says. The apostle Paul wrote: "Wives, submit to your husbands, as is fitting in the Lord" (Col. 3:18).

CHAPTER 7

My Advice to Younger Guys

For younger men who are also considering marrying older ladies, it is important that you take to the advice I am about to offer you.

1. Do not marry her for what she has. In most cases, guys who agree to marry older ladies are enticed and carried away by the substances the older ladies possess. This is common among celebrities; they are wealthy, famous, highly connected and they possess huge properties. Some younger guys prefer such ladies because of what they would get from them. They pretend to be nice, responsible, and altruistic, until they have achieved their aims. They are gold-diggers; they make sure they loot the ladies and leave them with little or nothing to fall back to.

This must not be said of you as a Christian. Such people will surely incur the wrath of God. Do not let your reason for marrying the lady be for the purpose of using her to achieve your selfish ambitions. You must relate with her with all sincerity and honesty. Let your motivation for accepting to marry her be because you love her from your heart. Sincerity pays the greatest dividend.

2. **Be sure lust is not what is driving you into the relationship**. Some ladies, though are of age, they still look charming, pretty, smart and elegant. You will be surprised to know what their ages are when you see how smart and graceful they are. They can quickly

catch the fancies of many young men. Therefore, be sure you are not driven by lust for their beauties, their positions, and they possessions.

Lust never satisfies; it doesn't give lasting gratification. If lust is what is driving you into the relationship, I promise you in a matter of time, you will regret the choice you make to marry her. Always remember that if love is a dream, marriage is the alarm clock.

3. **Don't you ever say you are doing her a favour by marrying her.** Never you let words like "you better thank your star I married you", "you better be grateful to me for marrying a cougar like you", "I shouldn't have married you if not that I pitied you", "you are so lucky to marry a young man like me", and so forth proceed out of your mouth.

You have not done her any favour by marrying her. She is as important as you are and you need each other to survive. You must see her as a blessing to your life. She is an asset and not a liability. She is a plus and not a minus. Do not mistreat her nor oppress her. She is very precious in the sight of God.

4. Do not compare her with anyone. The temptations of wanting to compare your older lady to other ladies may arise when conflict ensues in the home or when she's unable to meet some of your expectations. She will certainly not be able to meet all your expectations, just as you cannot meet all her expectations too. Another thing that may want to bring about comparison between her and younger ladies is when both of you do not share common social preferences.

In such a situation, you must avoid comparing her with anyone else. Accept her and love her for who she is. Just as she cannot meet all your expectations, I doubt if a younger lady will be able to meet all of them too. She is unique; she also has good things to offer. She is full of potentials and possibilities.

5. Make sure she's God's will for you. You must be willing to accept and follow God's will for your life. Following God's will for you should not be limited to marriage. It must cut across every aspect of your life—job, career, finance, marriage, position, parenting, ministry, etc. God's will for you is always good, acceptable and perfect (Rom.12:1-2).

Therefore, it is important that you ensure that she is the will of God for you. If the marriage is God's will for you, it is God's business to keep. He will supply the strength you both need to move on. He gives grace to prosper in His will. Just ensure that you are in the will of God. Though storms may rise against you, He will surely see you through.

Chapter 8

Now that you've decided to marry each other

I strongly believe that success in marriage is never automatic but *workmatic*. In other words, you have to work diligently at the success of your marriage. Therefore, I shall briefly itemize some of the nugget points that I strongly believe will lead to the success of your marriage. They are the final advice I want to offer you in this book, and if you keep to these advice, they will not only make your marriage succeed, they will make your home a place to be. Therefore, if you want your marriage to succeed, I advise to do the following:

1. Make God your priorities.

2. Make reading and studying the Word of God your daily responsibilities. This is my daily Bible study rule: No Bible no breakfast, no Scripture no sleep.

3. Determine to submit yourselves to the authority of God's Word in every decision you both have to make.

4. Do not go to bed with an unresolved conflict. Make sure you settle every conflict before you retire for the day.

5. Spend time to pray together. Daily family devotion should not be compromised. The family that prays together stays together.

6. Respect each other's opinions. Give each other the opportunity to contribute and to

express what each one feels about any decision you want to make in the home.

7. Avoid secrecy. Secrecy is not healthy for a Christian marriage; avoid it!

8. As much as possible, avoid the blame game. Do not blame your partner for whatever goes wrong in the family.

9. Learn to listen to whatever your partner has to say.

10. Help each other to achieve your daily, monthly or yearly goals or any goal you are pursuing.

11. Do not yell at each other. It creates resistance between couples.

12. Talk freely about your needs.

13. Be altruistic.

14. Be sensitive and empathetic.

15. Be generous to each other.

16. Find delight in holding hands together publicly.

17. Do household chores together.

18. Ensure you protect each other's interest.

19. Forgive each other as quick as possible.

20. Ensure you do not forget each other's birthday, wedding anniversary or any notable day in your lives. Celebrate each other on such days.

21. Exchange gifts with each other.

22. Appreciate each other both privately and publicly.

23. Deliberately punctuate your yearly activities to go for vacation together.

24. Avoid making offensive remarks when conflict ensues between you.

25. Do not find it difficult to say "I am sorry" whenever you are wrong.

26. Plan your finances together.

27. Cuddle and kiss each other often.

28. Send love text messages to each other always.

29. Avoid every form of vulgarity in your conversations.

30. You must always remember that every successful marriage requires a deaf husband and a blind wife.

31. Do not allow any conflict or disagreement to survive till the next day (I am repeating this point because it is fundamental).

32. Remember failed marriages usually have a bad effect on the society.

33. Don't be over possessive of each other.

34. Adopt each other's families (parents and siblings). In other word, his family becomes your family and her family becomes yours too.

On the final note, God must never be out of the picture if you both desire to have a blissful marital experience. Make Him the Alpha and the Omega of your marriage.

Perhaps you are married and your marriage is falling apart; you have tried all you could to keep things together, but you keep seeing your efforts becoming futile; I will like to introduce you to the greatest and incomparable marriage mender. His name is JESUS. He can heal your broken-heart, restore love and peace to your home, deliver your spouse from drugs and porno- addiction, help you bring order to your dysfunctional marriage, and ultimately, He wants to save your soul from hell.

If you confess with your mouth that Jesus is Lord, and believe in your heart that God raised Him from the dead, you will be saved. Are you ready to surrender your life, your marriage, your career and everything about you to Him? Then say this prayer with me: *Lord Jesus, I thank you for your love for me and for shedding your blood on the cross to save me. Jesus, today, I confess you with my mouth that you are my Lord and Saviour, and I believe that God raised you from the dead. Jesus, save my soul, save my marriage, and make me yours forever. Thank you for saving me. Amen!*

If you have said this prayer, I congratulate you. You are saved. I advise you to locate a Bible believing Church you can attend if you do not belong to any, give yourself to prayers daily, and make your Bible your daily companion.

Furthermore, I will like to hear from you. Please be kind enough to share your testimony with me, as this will help me to include you in my prayer list.

OTHER BOOKS BY THE AUTHOR

Careless Wives, Unfaithful Husbands.

List Price
Kindle: $2.99
Paperback: $8.00
ISBN-13:978-1537441818
Available at
www.amazon.com
BISAC: Family &
Relationships/ Marriage & Long Term Relationship

The Absurdities of Faith: Understanding Faith in its Rational and Irrational Sense.

Available in Kindle and Paperback Format. Visit www.amazon.com/author/ebenezerafolabi to place an order.

Other titles include:

A Closer Walk with Jesus

Doing Apologetics with an African Mindset

Making Apologetics Appealing to Africans

Bible and the Postmodern Man.

Visit the link below to place an order:
www.amazon.com/author/ebenezerafolabi.

Words from the Author

Thank you for taking your time to read this book. God bless you real good.

If this book has been a blessing to you and you feel like sharing your experience with the author or you need additional help, you can contact the author through the contact information below. Your personal comments and testimonies will be greatly appreciated. Perhaps you are also interested in translating this book to your language so that those who speak the language can also benefit from it, kindly contact the author through the contact information below for a discussion on that.

POSTAL ADDRESS:
Foursquare Gospel Church
210, Ebute Ojora Street,
Ebute Road, Ibafo,
Ogun State, Nigeria.
Email: ebenezerafolabi54@gmail.com.
Telephone Number: +2348160525695
Facebook: www.facebook.com/damilola.afolabi

Notes

CHAPTER 1—DOES AGE REALLY MATTER?

1. https://en.wikipedia.org/wiki/Age_disparity_in_sexual_relationships (Accessed in October, 2016).

2. http://www.scientificamerican.com/article/what-is-the-best-age-difference-for-husband-and-wife (Accesses in October, 2016).

3. https://en.wikipedia.org/wiki/Age_disparity_in_sexual_relationships (Accessed in October, 2016).

4. https://newrepublic.com/article/119282/science-does-not-support-rule-seven-relationships (Accessed in October, 2016).

5. http://www.scientificamerican.com/article/what-is-the-best-age-difference-for-husband-and-wife (Accessed in October, 2016).

CHAPTER 3—IS BIBLE IN SUPPORT OF WMYM?

1. Elimelech Westreich. *Levirate Marriage in the state of Israel: Ethnic Encounter and Challenge of a Jewish State,* 2003-2004, Vol. 37 *Is.L.R.* 428.

2. http://www.blainerobison.com/hebroots/levirate.htm (Accessed in October, 2016).

Made in the USA
Las Vegas, NV
02 December 2021